DO SOMETHING for SOMEONE ELSE

Written by **Loll Kirby**
Illustrated by **Yas Imamura**
Foreword by **Michael Platt**

MAGIC CAT PUBLISHING

Calling all activists!

Hello, I'm Michael.

I started working to tackle childhood hunger when I was eleven years old, and since then I've given away thousands of cupcakes and meals through my baking business and non-profit organisation.

There are some big problems in our world today. You may feel intimidated when you learn about them and uncertain what to do, but each of these problems can be solved by everyday people doing what they can.

The children in this book teach us that when each of us does something to face a problem we are passionate about we can change the world together.

Our world is a wonderful place and the future of it starts with you. So, look around you and do something for someone else... today!

MICHAEL PLATT
Food justice advocate and creator of Michael's Desserts

In this book, meet 12 real-life children...

Pupils from Sant Jordi primary school, Spain

Responsible for bringing people together in the community to prevent loneliness

Marie-Astrid from France

Passionate ballet dancer on a mission to make ballet inclusive

Christopher and Reece from South Africa

Two friends raising awareness of mental health through swimathons

Kesz from the Philippines

Protects children living on the streets through his organisation Championing Community Children

Havana from the USA

Fundraises to get children reading stories featuring Black characters

Winter from Australia

Founder of a fundraising programme that provides clean-water filter systems

Selin from Turkey

Inventor of robotic dogs to provide support for blind people

Katie from the USA

Creator of community gardens that feed people in need

Emily from the UK

Campaigner for accessibility on behalf of disabled people

Mohamad from Syria

Built a school in his refugee camp to help educate children

Elena from Germany

Shares violin performances on social media to inspire musicians

Yuqiu from China

Provides medical care to vulnerable people who are ill or injured

We're doing something to bring young and older people together...

The children at Sant Jordi primary school in Spain wanted to find ways to spend time with older people in their community. Older people can feel lonely if they have retired from their jobs so the children decided to invite a group to talk, play and spend time together working in their orchard. The project has developed over the years; they now work together with technology and hope other local schools will get involved soon.

Being invited along to an organised activity makes a big difference to someone who is lon... as it can be difficult to reach out to others

Millions of older people live alone, with no friends or family nearby.

Loneliness can affect anyone of any age, but older people are particularly vulnerable.

Spending time together is a great way to keep skills, stories and traditions alive, and children can learn from older people.

Children tend to talk a lot and have lots of questions and energy, so provide a natural relief from loneliness.

At Sant Jordi, older people teach the children how to grow tomatoes.

NAME: Sant Jordi primary school
COUNTRY: Spain
CHANGEMAKER FOR: Preventing loneliness in older people

GLORIA'S
STORE

I'm doing something to
protect children living
on the streets...

There are many
millions of
children who live
on the streets
for some or all
of the time.

Kesz replaces the bandages
on a child's arm to help
keep their wounds clean.

Kesz had a very difficult start in life and at the age of four he was living on the streets in the Philippines. When a social worker supported Kesz after an accident, he was given food, clothes and was able to go to school. But he didn't forget what his life had been like before, so on his birthday asked for sandals to give to children living on the streets. This one simple act grew into an organisation called Championing Community Children, set up by Kesz himself.

NAME: Kesz Valdez
COUNTRY: Philippines
CHANGEMAKER FOR:
Protecting children living on the streets

Children living on the streets do not always have access to a doctor so can get very ill.

Teaching children life skills helps them prepare for their future.

It can be hard for children living on the streets to stay healthy. Something small like a toothbrush can make a big difference.

Children living on the streets will hopefully find safe homes, but they need care and support in the meantime.

I'm doing something to help all children see themselves in a book...

Havana from the USA is passionate about children being able to see themselves in books. At the age of seven she started a fundraiser for her church choir's book club, Rhymers are Readers, to give out books to Black children which featured Black characters. Havana speaks out about many issues, particularly education for girls around the world, and understands the importance of reading in education. She believes that all children, regardless of their race, gender and circumstances, should have the same opportunities to learn and grow, and even change the world.

When we read books, we connect the events, emotions, experiences and characters in the books with ourselves.

Children who read are happier, healthier and more creative.

Havana shares some of her favourite books from the book club.

SPACE GIRL

GIRL BOSS

GIRL RESID

LITTLE ONE

ALL OF US

Stories bring joy, but if children never see characters that look like them, it can be harder for them to feel the same connection.

The number of books featuring Black characters is far smaller than the number of Black people in society.

Books act as mirrors to reflect our own lives, but also as windows so we can understand the lives of others.

space cat

SUPER RUBY

CHANGE THE WORLD

NAME: Havana Chapman-Edwards
COUNTRY: USA
CHANGEMAKER FOR: Diversity in children's books

I'm doing something to provide clean drinking water...

When Australian surfer Winter found out that people were drinking dirty water, he decided to do something, even though he was only nine at the time. Winter began to raise funds to buy water filters and made a trip to the Indonesian Mentawai Islands, where clean water is in short supply. His next step was to start working on his own fundraising programme called Surf to School, which encourages children to come to school dressed in surfing clothes in return for a donation to the cause.

One in ten people around the world don't have access to clean drinking water close to their home.

Water filters are a simple and effective way of purifying water so that people don't have to travel long distances to find it.

Clean drinking water is important for a healthy life and you can get ill very quickly without it.

The water filters have a syringe for cleaning when they clog or slow down, so they last a long time.

We don't just need clean water to drink, but also for keeping our bodies and our homes hygienic.

Winter helps to install the clean-water filter system.

NAME: Winter Vincent
COUNTRY: Australia
CHANGEMAKER FOR:
Providing clean drinking water

I'm doing something to create equal opportunities in ballet...

Marie-Astrid is a French ballet dancer who began dancing at five years old. Ballet is an art form that has not always felt open to everyone. Marie-Astrid dances with a company called Ballet Black, whose mission is to make ballet inclusive by supporting and celebrating Black and Asian dancers. They worked with a shoe manufacturer called Freed to create ballet shoes in brown and bronze shades, in addition to the pink colour that was used in the past.

Ballet is very physically demanding and ballet dancers are some of the strongest athletes and performers you will see.

Marie-Astrid leaps across the room in ballet shoes that match her skin tone.

The staple pink ballet shoes are a reminder of ballet's lack of diversity.

Before ballet shoes in brown and bronze shades, dancers had to use a technique called 'pancaking' to cover their shoes with make-up to match their skin tone.

Everyone should be able to see themselves represented fairly and equally in society.

The colour of your skin doesn't make any difference to how good you might become as a ballet dancer, but you might not know that ballet was worth considering if you'd never seen anyone like you doing it.

NAME: Marie-Astrid Mence
COUNTRY: France
CHANGEMAKER FOR:
Encouraging the next generation of young Black ballet dancers

I'm doing something to provide technology to help others...

When eleven-year-old Selin from Turkey learned how to build a robot, she used her interest in animals to develop her own models. Selin started by building a simple robotic dog. She understood that dogs provided love and companionship, and are also helpful with daily tasks for blind people. The latest version of Selin's robotic dog can now sit, bark and lie down and while it only understands English at the moment, her aim is to teach it more languages soon.

Selin teaches her friend to program the robotic dog to guide him across the park.

A robotic dog can enable a blind person to live independently removing barriers to daily tasks such as crossing the road.

NAME: Selin Örnek
COUNTRY: Turkey
CHANGEMAKER FOR:
Using robotics to help blind people

The robotic dogs are equipped with sensors that help them guide their owners.

Featuring image and voice recognition, each owner can programme their robotic dog.

Like any dog, the robotic dogs become much-loved friends, and offer loyalty and companionship.

253 million people worldwide are visually impaired, and 36 million of those people are blind.

I'm doing something to help feed people in need...

Katie, from the USA, started to grow fruit and vegetables at nine years old. After she grew an enormous cabbage from a tiny seedling, Katie donated it to a local soup kitchen where it fed 275 people. This inspired her to set up Katie's Krops which now has 100 gardens growing across the country. Young gardeners are taught how to start and maintain a successful garden and to donate the fresh produce to feed people in need.

Fruit and vegetables are packed with vitamins and minerals which help our bodies stay healthy.

Guidelines suggest that we should eat at least five portions of fruit and vegetables every day.

Plants which are used to the weather conditions in your area will be the easiest to grow.

NAME: Katie Stagliano
COUNTRY: USA
CHANGEMAKER FOR:
Growing a healthy end to hunger

Almost all plants can be grown in raised beds.

Fresh produce can be more expensive than packaged and processed food which means some people can't afford to eat it very often.

Katie donates the freshly picked produce.

LETTUCE

CARROTS

CABBAGE

KATIE'S KROPS

TOMATOES

It is obvious to see that some people are disabled because of the equipment they use.

Sometimes the way people are disabled is hard to see, such as learning difficulties.

Disabled people have the same rights to opportunities as everyone else, but often face barriers because they need to do some things differently.

Emily reads her comic book featuring disabled superheroes.

I'm doing something to support the lives of disabled people...

Thirteen-year-old Emily from the UK campaigns on behalf of disabled people. Emily was born with multiple health conditions and has used a wheelchair since she was three. As a result of the challenges she faced, she wanted to help create a world where everyone feels included. She has advised organisations on how to make parks easily accessible, and is creating a comic book with her dad about disabled superheroes.

NAME: Emily White
COUNTRY: UK
CHANGEMAKER FOR: Supporting and campaigning for disabled people

It's important to be kind and to embrace our differences.

Everybody has a right to access and safely use public places, such as shops, restaurants, cinemas and parks.

We're doing something to support young people's mental health...

After realising that their friends were suffering in silence, twelve-year-olds Christopher and Reece from South Africa took action. Christopher's passion for swimming led them to run twelve-hour swimathons to show how mental health issues can feel like a continuous struggle, but can become easier to manage with help. The money raised is used by the organisation they've set up, Swim For Change, to introduce mental health strategies in schools.

Christopher and Reece celebrate after a long, tiring swim.

SWIM FOR CHANGE

Making sure you have time to sleep, eat well, exercise and relax can help improve your mental health.

The term mental health describes how we're feeling and how well we can cope with challenges.

Mental health can change from moment to moment, day to day, or month to month.

Looking after your mental health is just as important as looking after your physical health.

Talking to people who care about you can be good for your mental health.

NAME: Christopher Kleynhans and Reece Slade

COUNTRY: South Africa

CHANGEMAKER FOR: Raising awareness of mental health issues

I'm doing something to educate children who had to leave their homes...

At the age of twelve, Mohamad had to flee Syria, where he was born, when it became too dangerous. Mohamad and his family escaped to a refugee camp in Lebanon, where Mohamad could no longer go to school, so he set out to make a difference for children in the same situation. He built a school in the refugee camp and began teaching maths and photography, and soon others came to help teach as well.

A refugee is someone who has left their country because of a dangerous situation and cannot return home safely.

NAME: Mohamad Al Jounde
COUNTRY: Syria
CHANGEMAKER FOR: Education for refugee children

Over half of refugees are children.

A refugee will travel to a a new country where they hope to have a chance to keep learning and working hard, as they did before.

Schools are places that bring people together to educate and learn.

When people flee their homes, they often have to leave behind their families and friends.

Mohamad teaches the children how to use a camera to take a photo.

I'm doing something to inspire children to share their love of music...

At just eleven years old, Elena from Germany was accepted into Hanze University as their youngest ever violinist. She was so dedicated that she had reached the same standard as musicians many years older than her, and the following year she performed on a television talent show called Superkids. Elena shares her love of music by posting her practice and performance videos on social media to inspire young musicians watching from around the world.

Music has many benefits for our health and happiness, and there are lots of different instruments you can try, including your own voice.

It's easier to put lots of effort into doing something that really interests you, so find your passion and focus your energy there.

Music can be used as a way to express yourself without the need for words.

Elena plays a piece on the violin as the audience rises to its feet to give a standing ovation!

Learning to play music is good for your brain, and can help you do better at school.

The more you practise playing and creating music, the better you'll be.

I'm doing something to help people who are ill or injured...

Yuqiu was just fourteen years old when she was injured under rubble in the Wenchuan mega-earthquake in her home country of China.
Once Yuqiu recovered, she decided to help others in the way that she herself had been helped. Yuqiu now works as a nurse in hospitals and doctors' surgeries, as well as visiting patients in remote villages when they are unable to leave their home.

Remote areas have a large number of older people — often with long-term illnesses and who are disabled — who cannot travel long distances for medical care.

A nurse is trained to give care to people to help them stay healthy and even to save their lives.

NAME: Yuqiu Chen
COUNTRY: China
CHANGEMAKER FOR:
Providing medical care to vulnerable people

For some patients, a conversation with a nurse is their only contact with the outside world, so the visits are important for their mental health and happiness.

...ons of people live ...mote areas that are ...nerable to disasters ...ch as earthquakes.

Yuqiu listens carefully as her patient describes his symptoms.

Nursing training takes years of study and dedication.

How can you help to do something for someone else?

Studies suggest that we feel less connected to others now than we did in the past — adults' jobs require longer hours, people travel further distances for study and work, and technology enables us to complete daily tasks without human interaction. But feeling part of a group — whether that be family, friends, school or a club — is important to our health and happiness. Helping others can bring us closer to them, meaning that everyone benefits from us taking action to spread kindness wherever we can.

1. Help others by being polite and respectful when you talk to them. We can learn from the people around us about their lives and experiences if we ask questions and listen carefully to the answers.

2. Inspire others by finding a hobby you are passionate about. A hobby is a great way to meet people who have the same interests as you. Share your passion with as many people as possible to inspire them to join in, too.

3. Provide a listening ear to someone who has a problem. Offer help if they ask for it, but don't feel that you always need to rush to find a solution for them, because sometimes we just need to get our worries off our chest.

4. Create art to bring joy to those around you. It might be through music, writing, dancing or anything that you enjoy, but expressing ourselves in these ways can invite others to connect and share their experiences.

5. Bring people together to increase their happiness. Take practical action, like hosting a gathering for neighbours living alone, or organising a sale of second-hand items at your school.

6. Support your family by helping out at home. It makes everyone's lives easier if the cooking, cleaning and other jobs are shared around and you're likely to learn some valuable skills along the way!

7. Improve your school by joining the student council and sharing your ideas. If you put yourself forward and talk to others about the causes that mean something to you, you can start to make changes.

8. Protect the environment around where you live by reducing, reusing and recycling. There are plenty of steps we can take to look after our planet and if we encourage others to do the same then the impact will be even greater.

9. Educate yourself about important issues, such as racism and inequality. We can find out about how we can change things in the world through learning and sharing our knowledge with others.

10. Share with others so that everyone has enough of what they need. Many of us consume more than our fair share of resources, which leaves less for others. If we are thoughtful and kind, we can share things more equally.

Ten things you can do to make a difference to someone else:

1. Start small and build from there. Look out for people struggling at school or in your neighbourhood and think about how you could help them.

2. Join together with people who are working towards the same thing as you. Teamwork can make big tasks more manageable.

3. Share your plans with teachers, newspapers or magazines. They can help spread your ideas even further and get people interested in your plans.

4. Stay up to date with local and global news. Watching, listening to and reading the news can help you decide who needs the most help.

5. Create a petition. This is a good way to demonstrate that a large number of people care about the same thing and would like to see a change.

6. Set up a crowdfunding campaign for your cause. Lots of people donating a little bit of money can make a big difference.

7. Speak out at every opportunity. Encouraging conversation can start the process of change and you will learn by listening to others.

8. Be an active member of your community. Joining local groups means you'll meet new people and learn about what's important to them.

9. Seek out volunteering opportunities. Giving up your time for a cause you believe in can be very rewarding and helps others.

10. Write to your local member of parliament or your local council. Councillors and politicians are able to effect bigger change.

Further reading

With the help of an adult, find out more about the children and issues featured in this book on these websites:

do-it.org

dosomething.org

actionforhappiness.org

michaelsdesserts.com

kidsrights.org

womenyoushouldknow.net

wintervincent.com

balletblack.co.uk

digitalgirlaward.com

katieskrops.com

departmentofability.com

swimforchange.co.za

LOLL KIRBY has spent many years being inspired by young people, through her work as a primary school teacher and forest school leader. She believes that children have the best ideas and that they're never too small to start making a difference. Loll likes kindness, dark chocolate buttons and spotting interesting clouds while out running in Leamington Spa, where she lives with her family. Loll wrote this book, as well as her first book, Old Enough to Save the Planet, for anyone who wants to make positive changes in the world.

YAS IMAMURA is a Filipino-American illustrator. As a migrant, Yas has a personal understanding of what small acts of kindness and solidarity can do to empower a community and bring people together. Her greeting card company, Quill & Fox, has also given her the opportunity to create moments of thoughtfulness for others — how a piece of folded art can bridge distances in ways our modern devices can't. Yas has always been fond of doodling and much of her work draws inspiration from the books she enjoyed as a child, her art evolving into a mixture of the timeless and modern.

MICHAEL PLATT has been baking since he was nine years old, but has been interested in the challenges of inequality since he learned about the historic March on Washington at the age of six. Inspired by a pair of shoes he received as a present, Michael began a baking business, Michael's Desserts, with a one-for-one model where he donates a dessert to someone in need for every dessert that he sells. Michael is now a fourteen-year-old social entrepreneur, food justice advocate and believer that we should all do something for someone else.

MAGIC CAT PUBLISHING

Do Something for Someone Else © 2021 Magic Cat Publishing Ltd
Written by Loll Kirby • Foreword by Michael Platt
Illustrations © 2021 Yas Imamura • Text © 2021 Magic Cat Publishing
First Published in 2021 by Magic Cat Publishing Ltd
Unit 2 Empress Works, 24 Grove Passage, London E2 9FQ, UK
This paperback edition first published 2022

A catalogue record for this book is available from the British Library.

ISBN 978-1-913520-68-7

The illustrations were painted using gouache and watercolour • Set in Rainer and Panforte Pro

Published by Rachel Williams and Jenny Broom
Designed by Nicola Price • Edited by Helen Brown

The publication is not authorised, licensed or approved by any of the children featured in this book.

Manufactured in Lithuania, BAL0122

9 8 7 6 5 4 3 2 1

FSC
www.fsc.org
MIX
Paper from responsible sources
FSC® C107574